A GUIDE T
NAVAJO
SANDPAINTINGS

by Mark Bahti

with Eugene Baatsoslanii Joe

RIO NUEVO PUBLISHERS

AN IMPRINT OF TREASURE CHEST BOOKS

TUCSON, ARIZONA

ACKNOWLEDGMENTS

To our fathers, in grateful appreciation for all they have shared with us.

We wish to acknowledge the assistance of many people, including Herbert Beenhouwer, Nelson Begay, Ed Foutz, Jed Foutz, Georgianna Kennedy Simpson, Jack Fowler, James C. Joe Sr., Russ Lingruen, Scott Ryerson, John Tanner, Amber Wolcott, Vince Ferrari, Joe Ben Sr., and Tom Wheeler. Special recognition must be given to those who had the foresight to preserve Navajo ceremonial knowledge for future generations, heeding the D'ginneh who warned of disastrous consequences if the religious knowledge of the Diné is not kept alive: especially Father Berard Haile, Hosteen Klah, Franc Newcomb, Leland C. Wyman, Slim Curly, Frank Mitchell, Gladys Reichard, and Miguelito. The work of such contemporary scholars as David M. Brugge, Charlotte Frisbie, David McAllester, Jerrold E. Levy, Paul G. Zolbrod, James C. Faris, and John Farella carries on what their predecessors began and enlightens us as much about the human condition as it does the Navajo mind.

Rio Nuevo Publishers ™
P. O. Box 5250
Tucson, AZ 85703-0250
(520) 623-9558, www.rionuevo.com

ISBN 1-887896-05-8

Title page sandpainting of yé'ii by Joe Ben Jr.
Photographs of Daniel Smith at work are by W. Ross Humphreys. Others are by David Burckhalter and Photographic Works.

This book is set in Bitstream Charter and ITC Goudy Sans types.
Edited by Linnea Gentry
Printed in Korea

We wish to especially thank Rosie Yellowhair and Joe E. Tanner Jr. of Fifth Generation Trading Company for loan of the sandpaintings found on pages 20, 32, 52, and 58. We would also like to thank Hogback Trading for the sandpainting on page 56, Kennedy Indian Arts for the image on page 43, Arroyo Trading for the Eugene B. Joe image on page 10 and the Joe Ben Jr. images on the title page and pages 14, 15, 24, 25, 26, 28, 33, 38, 39, 44, and 61, and Shiprock Trading for the others.

TABLE OF CONTENTS

Song of the Sun Creation

They emerged, they say he is planning it.
They emerged, they say he is planning it.
They emerged, they say he is planning it.
The sun will be created, they say he is planning it.
Its face will be blue, they say he is planning it.
Its eyes will be black, they say he is planning it.
Its chin will be yellow, they say he is planning it...
Its strength is dangerous, they say he is planning it.
The sacred words will be created,
they say he is planning it.

—from the Navajo Creation Story

Yé'ii Bichaii dancers in a winter ceremony

Sandpainting is a somewhat misleading word for an art that, as traditionally practiced, utilizes crushed dried plants as well as crushed stone. Drypainting is perhaps a more accurate term and is one applied to images created on the ground out of earth or plant matter in other parts of the world as well, ranging from the mandalas made by Tibetan Buddhists, to those recounting creation stories made by native Australians, to those made on certain Christian holy days in Latin America. Many of the tribes of the Great Plains of North America also utilized drypaintings in their rituals, such as the famous Sun Dance. Here in the American Southwest, groups such as the Pueblo Indians of the Rio Grande Valley of New Mexico, the Hopi of northern Arizona, and the Tohono O'odham of the Sonoran Desert make or have made ritual drypaintings as well as the Navajo people of the Four Corners region. Yet however technically inaccurate the term may be, sandpainting is how these unique works of religious art have been most popularly labeled.

In the language of the Navajo* (the **Diné**, which means "the People"), a sandpainting is **ikaah**, which is perhaps best translated as a summoning of the gods. The Navajos, like many other tribes in the Southwest, feel that if a prayer is offered correctly, down to the smallest detail and with a good heart, the deity or deities must answer it. They are compelled to do so. If they do not answer, it was because the offering or ritual was imperfect in some way. The presence of these Holy People, called upon in the proper ritual context by these images, forms the heart of Navajo religious belief.

According to the Navajos, the universe is a very delicately balanced system, full of enormously powerful forces with potential for both good and evil. If the balance of the universe is upset even unintentionally, a disaster, usually in the form of an illness, will result. Furthermore, the Navajos believe that only

---

* The Navajo language has been undergoing the process of transcription for only about a hundred years. Different systems still appear in various publications about the Navajos and their culture. One problem in introducing Navajo words to English speakers is the difficulty in both the spelling and the pronunciation of a tonal language. The system used in this book follows that developed by Robert Young and William Morgan as presented in *Colloquial Navajo: A Dictionary* and in *Navajo-English Dictionary* by Leon Wall and William Morgan.

humans can upset the balance. Kicking over an anthill, building a campfire with wood from a tree struck by lightning, or crossing the path of a bear without offering it a prayer of respect are enough to upset the state of harmony, the balance that the Navajos call **hozhon**. The nature of the affront or transgression will determine the type of illness. A traditional Navajo who becomes ill will obtain the services of a "hand trembler" to determine the cause and prescribe the cure. Painful joints may point to the bear as the cause and the Mountain Way as the appropriate ceremony for the cure. Partial paralysis may be due to violating a lightning-related taboo and require the Shooting Way.

The diagnostician does not perform the ceremony. That is done by a **hataałii**, commonly translated as "medicine man" but more analogous to a doctor in that he is a healer. In some texts he is referred to as a chanter or singer because of the prayers he chants during the ceremonies, which are called **xatal**, or "song ceremonials." (While Navajo society is matrilineal and most diagnosticians are

A Tohono O'odham sandpainting made for display at the Arizona-Sonora Desert Museum, in Tucson, in the 1970s. Photo by Mervin W. Larson.

women, most hataałii are men.) Variations in the ceremony depend upon the age and sex of the patient. Sun images are generally associated with male patients, moon images with female patients. The entire extended family and community gathers for the one- to nine-day ceremony in support of the patient.

Prayers, medicine tools, songs, herbs, as well as sandpainting images are used to heal the patient through a restoration of harmony. A portion of the immense and complex Navajo mythology that relates to the cause of the patient's illness is retold in word and image. Generally speaking, the story recalls some misfortune that befalls the hero of the story. In time and with help from others, often a **yé'ii** (a supernatural being or mythical hero), the hero recovers, learning the ceremony to heal such problems and to teach to others. One such story involves one of the Warrior Twins (the powerful heroes in many Navajo myths) who shot an animal with an arrow that had the wrong type of feather attached. The Thunder People captured the twin and took him to the Sky People, who reprimanded him and taught him ceremonies to cure those with illness caused by lightning. By identifying with a hero such as the Twin (who is one of those summoned by the sandpainting) and with the vital aid of the hataałii, the patient becomes stronger. Health and harmony are restored.

Sandpainting images require the careful attention of the hataałii, as a slight error could result in harm rather than a cure. The image itself, which must be started at sunrise and completed by sunset, can cause harm to those present. To prevent this from happening, the image is first "erased" with a wooden stick with prayer feathers attached. In some instances the sand on which the image has been created rests on a tarp in order to facilitate complete removal of the sand and image. The material is disposed of some distance from any home, trail, or corral. A final prayer is said over the remains, which some say "discharms" the sands.

Because the ceremonies are long and complex and the harm in doing them incorrectly is great, a hataałii begins his career as an apprentice to experienced masters. It may be years—a decade or more—before he is ready to practice. And some never do. The tremendous demand on a hataałii's time, among other factors, is why a number of ceremonies have died out. Only for the Blessing Way (see page 28) is the number of practitioners growing.

The history of sandpainting is an interesting one. Most ethnologists suggest that the Navajos probably learned their use from Pueblo Indians who had fled the Rio Grande Valley and taken refuge among the Navajos out of fear of

A yé'ii bichaii, a Navajo dancer who portrays
the yé'ii in various Navajo religious
ceremonies, by Eugene Baatsoslanii Joe

NAVAJO SANDPAINTING ARTIST Eugene Baatsoslanii Joe describes the ceremony this way:

The scene is as ancient as the Navajo people. The setting is the traditional Navajo hogan,* with Mother Earth for a floor and the entrance facing east. The elders of the tribe, sitting cross-legged, awaken the silence with the shaking of gourd rattles and the chanting begins.

The sun streams in through the smoke hole of the hogan, bathing the patient in its light. The chanting continues, unfolding the exploits of one of the heroes of Navajo legend. The sandpainting is done in a careful and sacred manner, according to the ancient knowledge of the art, with each figure and each design in order and done with the five sacred colors (white, blue, yellow, black, and red).

As the patient is seated atop the completed sandpainting, the hataałii bends to reverently touch a portion of a figure in the sandpainting, then moves to touch the patient, transferring the medicine and the power. As this is done, the sickness falls away from the patient and harmony returns. Then before the sun sets, the sandpainting is erased with a sacred feather staff and is swept onto a blanket to be carried outside and carefully disposed of. In casting the sand away, the last of the sickness is carried away from the patient who, now healed through faith, rises to "walk in beauty" once again.

---

* The word is spelled **hooghan** in the current Navajo system.

Spanish reprisals during the reconquest of New Mexico in 1692 (after the Great Pueblo Revolt of 1680). Although Pueblo use of sandpaintings in religious ceremonies is quite limited, the practice has evolved into a vastly more complex and important role among the Navajos. Sandpaintings play a major role in their religion, a belief system which medical doctors and modern hospitals that serve the Navajo people have also come to recognize. Medical staffs now accept that successful treatment of many traditional Navajo patients must be done in conjunction with the recommendations or prescriptions of a hataałii. The mind-body connection to wellness, long known to groups such as the Navajo, is only now gaining acceptance in Western medicine.

According to Navajo history, however, they were first instructed in the art of sandpainting by the Holy Ones, divine beings of tremendous power and importance never seen by human eyes. The Holy Ones became known through instructions they relayed to spirits, such as the Wind People, who passed on knowledge of the ceremonial songs to the ancient Navajos. Among the sacred knowledge given to the first apprentices during seven days and seven nights of purification and instruction were songs, prayers, medicine objects, plants with protective and curative powers, and sandpaintings. These originals were painted on scrolls made of mountain sheep skins. But the apprentices were told that they must do their own sandpaintings with sand on Mother Earth, a stipulation to prevent the knowledge from being hoarded and to ensure that anyone with the necessary ability and patience could learn them. As the Holy Ones told them:

We will not give you this picture.
Men are not as good as we;
They might quarrel over the picture and tear it
And that would bring misfortune.
The black cloud would not come again,
And the rain would not fall.
The corn would not grow.
But you may paint it on the ground,
With the colors of the earth.

—from the Navajo Creation Story

The FIRST APPEARANCE OF sandpainting images outside of religious use was in the article "Mythic Dry-Paintings of the Navajos" by Dr. Washington Matthews, which was published in *The American Naturalist* in 1884. Museums and art exhibits held demonstrations of sandpainting art, but permanent reproductions of sandpaintings were usually done in association with efforts to record Navajo ceremonial knowledge. Most were done by Anglo ethnologists and traders in watercolors or colored pencils on paper. A few Navajos also made such permanent images. The breaking of an important taboo—creating images that last longer than the prescribed daylight hours and that can be seen outside the permitted winter months (when snakes and lightning are asleep)—was a difficult barrier and is one that still exists. (As recently as 1998 the annual Navajo Studies Conference was moved to winter to allow discussion of topics that hataałii say should not be discussed at any other time.)

To prevent them from harm, many of the Navajos involved in these efforts took the precaution of undergoing the Blessing Way ceremony. Other practitioners felt they would be safe if the sandpainting images were not precisely accurate. Changes could be slight: substituting a prescribed color with another, leaving out one of the four sacred plants by duplicating one of the other three, or changing the number of feathers on the heads of Holy People. Whatever it was, the alteration had to be significant enough to avoid empowering the image and calling the gods.

Especially influential in legitimizing the recording and preservation of the ceremonies was the famed hataałii Klah (c.1867-1937), usually referred to with an honorific as Hosteen Klah. Klah was also the best-known weaver of sandpainting rugs, along with two of his nieces, although he was not the first. The first recorded sandpainting rug was woven for a member of the Wetherill Expedition in the Chaco Canyon area in 1896; there were no known repercussions for the weaver. However, the situation was quite different when Yanabah Simpson, Navajo wife of the trader who ran the Canyon Gallegos Trading Post southeast of Farmington, New Mexico, wove a rug with a yé'ii image shortly after the turn of the century. Dick Simpson proudly displayed his

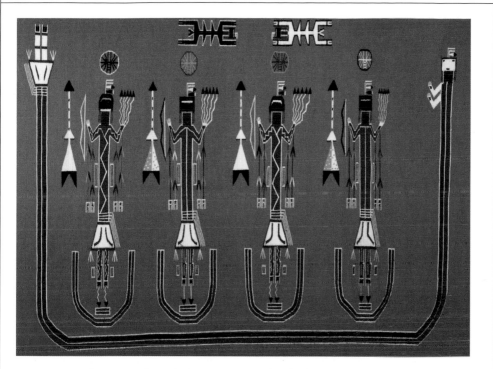

A rug depicting a line of yé'ii, woven sometime in the mid-twentieth century
by an unknown weaver

wife's first weaving in the trading post—to the immediate consternation of their Navajo clientele. Several Navajo men, including at least one hataałii, were so incensed that Simpson had to immediately remove it and put it in his vault. For a brief time the trader apparently even feared that someone might set fire to his post. The rug sold a short time later to an East Coast collector for $300 or more. This astounding sum was not lost on the Simpsons and other weavers in the area, despite the dire warnings of the hataałii. Yanabah wove at least three more before she died in 1912.

Sandpainting motifs as decorative art began in 1923 when the Fred Harvey Company built the Hotel Navajo in Gallup, New Mexico, in which architect Mary Coulter used twelve large sandpainting images on the interior walls. By the mid 1930s there was some experimentation—initially by non-Indian artists—with painting on a background made of sand glued to board.

Anglos George and Mae de Ville and David Villaseñor had also experimented with techniques to create permanent sandpaintings. Villaseñor even published a book on the subject, *How to Do Permanent Sandpaintings*, in 1972. It is doubtful whether any Navajos learned sandpainting from the book, but the images illustrated—and mislabeled—had an unfortunate legacy. In one example, Pollen Boy on the Sun was labeled "Sun and Eagle," an error still common on many sandpaintings.

THE NEW ART IS PASSED ON

The first Navajo to do the new type of permanent sandpainting was Fred Stevens (also known as Grey Squirrel) in the late 1950s. Stevens was from the tiny community of Sheep Springs on the east side of the Chuska Mountains not far south of Shiprock, New Mexico. Even today, most Navajo sandpainting artists can trace their family connections back to this area. Stevens, who demonstrated his art in Europe and Latin America under the sponsorship of the U.S. government, then taught Patsy and Francis Miller. (See Stevens' sandpaintings on pages 42 and 47.)

A deity from the Night Chant in a modern sandpainting by Joe Ben Jr.

The Joe family, which includes a number of sandpainters, is a good example of how the art of sandpainting is being taught and passed down today. Patriarch James C. Joe first began to study traditional sandpainting at age ten with his grandfather, who was instructing him in the Navajo religion. James Joe later became a medicine man. One of the most talented and well respected of his time, he knew a total of three Ways. His aunt, the wife of Francis Miller, introduced her nephew to sandpainting on boards in 1962. Joe went on to experiment with the new medium, making other improvements and developing his own techniques. As a former medicine man, his knowledge and respect for traditional Navajo beliefs are evident in his work. James Joe passed this knowledge on to many members of his family, including his son Eugene.

CREATING A SANDPAINTING

Sandpainting can be tedious and exacting work, requiring a great deal of preparation before the actual painting begins. As with most arts and crafts, besides the crucial matter of artistic vision, the more time spent at it and the more patient, experienced, and demanding the artisan, the better the final result. Its basic material is the rock.

Rocks are often important physical manifestations in Navajo myths and cosmology. All that remains of the monsters (**yé'ii tsoh**) destroyed by the mythical heroes, the Twins, now are rocks. The lava flow near Grants, New Mexico, for example, is the dried blood of one of these yé'ii tsoh. A winged yé'ii tsoh was turned to stone and became the famous landmark in northwestern New Mexico now called Shiprock. Interestingly, a few of these fearsome yé'ii tsoh to survive were Poverty, Sickness, and Death, who argued that it was necessary for them to survive in order to make room for the young. The Twins also allowed Lice to live, agreeing with his argument that without him people would not have an incentive to keep themselves clean.

A deity from the Night Chant in a modern sandpainting by Joe Ben Jr.

Tsé' Axe'tsa, or Crushing Rocks (also called Traveling Rocks), were among the monsters that plagued the Navajo people in the mythological past. When someone walked between them, they would clap together, killing the passer-by. One of the Warrior Twins, Monster Slayer (**Nayéé' Neezghání**), built a fire under the rocks and then struck them with his club,

AN EDUCATION IN SANDPAINTING

James Joe with son Eugene

IN THE FOLLOWING account, Eugene Baatsoslanii Joe describes how he first learned the art and then developed his own style:

The first stage of my education in sandpainting came from amusing myself as a young child with drawing. My tools were my fingers and the drawing surface was the desert sand covering Mother Earth. I had the glorious light from Father Sky to light my childish artistic attempts. Subject matter was no problem as there was the world of nature surrounding me to select from.

My father saw my interest, and thus began my formal instruction in traditional sandpainting under his patient tutelage. At first my tasks were menial: grinding the rocks of various colors, keeping the workshop clean, and preparing the boards for the paintings he did. Like most apprentices, I found the work tedious, but I quickly learned that they are a very necessary part of the whole procedure and would result in a beautiful creation. All forms of art demand discipline if pride in good craftsmanship is to be developed, and sandpainting is no exception.

Of course, physical labor was only one element in my instruction. I would carefully listen to my father's spiritual instruction, which was the most essential element. He instilled in me the feelings of reverence, pride, and beauty in the traditional sandpaintings. I worked under his guidance for twelve years. As I became older I sought out others, particularly artists (not exclusively Indian), who were willing to share their ideas and knowledge in order to enrich my training. My quest seemed insatiable: as I began to ally myself with these people, I found myself yearning to learn ever more. My friends were generous with their time and talents; I shall forever be indebted to them and to my father, my family, and my people. My greatest desire is to preserve this traditional native craft with all the reverence it deserves, indeed demands, and also to present it in a manner for all to receive pleasure from it.

shattering the pieces in all directions. The heat and the blow caused the stones to change color, becoming the rock that is now used in traditional sandpaintings.

Sandpainters gather most of this rock within the traditional (as opposed to the modern or legal) boundaries of Navajoland (**Dinétah**) and usually keep the exact locations of their sources a closely guarded secret. The desired rocks are usually dug or sledge hammered loose and then carried to the artist's home in buckets, where they are broken up into still smaller pieces and allowed to dry completely. The drying process is important, for the true color of a stone is revealed only after the last traces of moisture have evaporated. Once the pieces are fully dry, they are ground using a mano and metate, a mortar and pestle, or a hand-operated coffee grinder.

The five basic colors in sandpaintings are white, black, blue, yellow, and red. Blue is sometimes represented with a light gray sand. Traditional minerals include limestone, turquoise, vanadium, gypsum, azurite, and sandstone. The artist shown here is Daniel Smith.

As of the turn of the twenty-first century, a few individuals have experimented with commercially colored sands after attempts to color the sand with oil pigments proved unsatisfactory. Still others have begun to use a wider range of stones, including malachite, lapis lazuli, and verdite (minerals found far from Navajoland), even coral on occasion.

After grinding, the sand is sifted and strained into three grades of fineness: one for background material, the second for general fill, and the third and finest for delicate details and outlines. Any material that is too coarse is reground or discarded. Similarly the finest material—dust and powder that are difficult to control—is winnowed away, as it can easily "pollute" other colors during the process. Many artists are skipping this tedious and time-consuming procedure by purchasing ready-to-use sands from stores and trading posts, mostly in northwestern New Mexico. Dyed sands are available, but for the most part they have a readily noticeable artificial appearance.

Sheets of particleboard of ⅜-inch thickness (or ½-inch for large works) are the preferred surfaces. Early experiments with plywood proved less satisfactory. Some early works were done on tempered hardboard or masonite, and a few artists have gone back to using them. The boards are sawed into the desired sizes and shapes, and the edges sanded smooth.

Experiments with adhesives included casein, Duco (a combination of varnish and lacquer), and white glue, which is the preferred adhesive used by virtually all Navajo sandpainters working today. Each sandpainting artist prepares a white glue according to personal preference and spreads the mixture evenly over the entire surface. The glue becomes the base coat to hold the sand smoothly and evenly. The boards are placed outside in the sun or some other warm place to dry. Depending on the weather, drying may take several days. Afterwards the artist may lightly sand the surface to remove irregularities or buildup of glue, as it's important to have a smooth working surface.

Sandpainter Daniel Smith, who signs his pieces "Hosteen Etsitty," prepares the ground, stencils

Then the actual painting begins. The design is drawn in glue using fine brushes. To prevent the glue from drying before the sand can be applied, the artist separates the work into sections and completes only one section at a time. And to prevent the mixing of colors, the artist applies only one color of sand each time a section is prepared. While some sandpainters may pencil in the figures they plan to make, others will make only a few measurements and guides to ensure symmetry. Still others work almost entirely by eye.

The methods of applying sand vary, with each artist having his or her own technique. The most frequently used method is to cup a generous pinch of sand held by the second, third, and fourth fingers in the palm of the hand and then allow it to trickle out from a crook in the index finger, using the thumb to regulate the flow. The flow must be soft and even or the line will be distorted. If the glue is too thick, the build-up of sand will easily break off. If it is too thin, the line will be faint and indistinct and often blurred.

When completed, the sandpainting is allowed to dry for a day or two more. Then the entire surface is lightly sprayed with a fine mist of matte fixative or shellac to secure the sand.

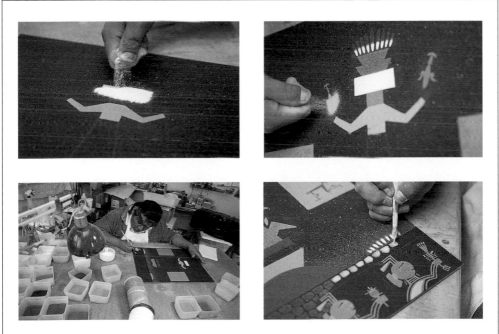

in the design, and applies the glue and then the sand for an elaborate Corn Mother image.

Errors or variations not accepted in traditional sandpaintings almost always appear in those made for sale. Knowledgeable Navajo sandpainting artists will often deliberately put in an "error" to prevent the exact copying of a religious sandpainting. Another will vary an element to make it visually more pleasing to the artist himself, while yet another not raised in traditional religion will make unintentional errors due to unfamiliarity with sandpainting imagery.

It is worth noting, however, that because of different cultural perspectives, what appears as a variation in a sandpainting to a non-Navajo may not be a variation at all to a Navajo. For example, a yé'ii may have either a blue or a green face. In this context both colors are identical, because the religious classification of color by purpose or direction sees them as interchangeable. The Navajos recognize blue and green as being different shades with different names; but since the colors have the same function or purpose ceremonially, they are considered to be the same with but one name in the context of religious art.

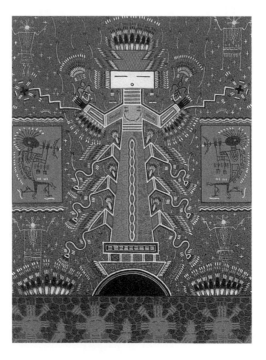

A completed Corn Mother sandpainting by Daniel Smith

THE SANDPAINTINGS

SONG OF THE MOON CREATION

They emerged, they say he is planning it.
They emerged, they say he is planning it.
They emerged, they say he is planning it.
The moon will be created, they say he is planning it.
Its face will be white, they say he is planning it.
Its chin will be yellow, they say he is planning it.
Its horns will be white, they say he is planning it....
Its strength is dangerous, they say he is planning it.
The sacred words will be created,
they say he is planning it.

—from the Navajo Creation Story

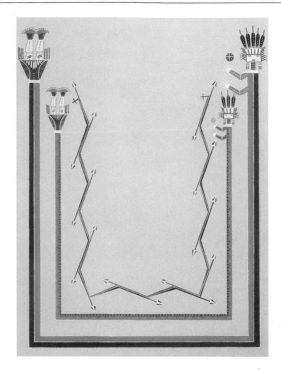

CEREMONIAL PROTECTION OF THE SANDPAINTING

WHEN A SANDPAINTING IS CREATED, the opening or entrance always faces east. This is the entrance through which the Holy People come to empower the image by their presence. East is a sacred direction, the one from which no harm or evil can enter. The other three sides, however, are vulnerable and must be protected by a (usually) continuous design element encircling the southern, western, and northern sides. The most frequently used motif is **Náóts'íílid**, the hermaphroditic rainbow deity.

Other protective garlands include: the mirage garland, which is a band of multi-colored dots; a rainbow with feathers representing prayer plumes at each end (and often at the two corners); interconnected arrows; or even simply three rainbow bars. Only a very few sandpaintings, notably those from the Blessing Way, do not use protective garlands.

NOTE: As in this example, all sandpaintings in this book are oriented with the eastern side at the top of the page unless noted otherwise.

GUARDIANS

THESE FIGURES GENERALLY APPEAR in pairs at the entrance (eastern edge) of the sandpainting. Their function—much like that of the garlands—is to give added protection to the sandpainting by guarding the opening. Illustrated here are some of the more common ones, all important personages or motifs from Navajo legends. Many also appear as major or central motifs in other sandpaintings. Beginning in the upper left corner and proceeding counter-clockwise: the sun (**jóhonaa'éí**) and moon (**tl'éhonaa'éí**), Big Fly (**Dontso**), a medicine bag (**jish**), Bat (**jaa'abaní**), a bow (**altíí**) and arrow (**k'aa'**), Otter (**tábaastíín**), and Snake (**tł'iish**).

Otter and Beaver are memorialized for helping the Twin War Gods when they went to visit their father the Sun. An entire Way (the Enemy Way), used for protection of those going into battle or purification of those just returned, is based on this story. Although they had made the long and perilous journey from the home of Changing Woman (their mother) to their father's home, overcoming many obstacles and dangers, Sun tested them further to be certain they were indeed his sons. In one test he hurled bolts of lightning at the boys. They were saved by the skins given them by Otter and Beaver.

Dontso usually travels on the shoulder or behind the ear of the hero of a story. From here he can observe events, warn the hero of danger, and instruct him how to obtain help from the gods when necessary. Big Fly is believed to be based in part on a type of tachinid fly that seems to prefer alighting on peoples' heads or shoulders.

MUCH HAS BEEN MADE of the different categories of beings in Navajo religion, but the Navajos themselves have only three categories. First are the yé'iis. These include any and all supernatural beings (that is, those with more power

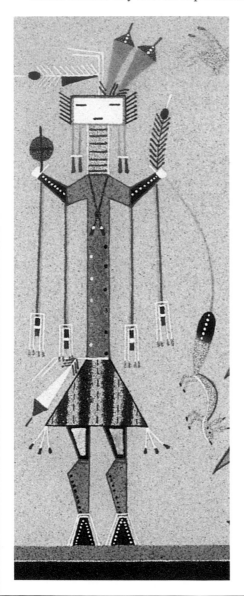

than humans) from Navajo religion, although the word is usually translated as "god." They are unable to speak and therefore are called **hashch-eeh**, which means "the speechless ones." Other groups of deities include the **diyinii** or Holy People, a group (some say twelve) of divine entities who may or may not be kindly disposed towards humans, and **xactce hastye**, sometimes translated as "persuadables," who are particularly helpful to humans.

The masked dancers who portray the yé'ii in certain ceremonies are commonly called yé'ii bichaii dancers after the nine-night Yé'ii Bichaii ceremony of the Night Way in which they appear. Yé'ii Bichaii is also a name for Talking God, one of the Holy People.

Although there are exceptions to the rule (see the images of Father Sky and Mother Earth on pages 26 and 27), a round head indicates a male yé'ii and a square or rectangular head indicates a female yé'ii. In ritual images, the female body is white with a red outline, while the male is black or white with a red outline. All yé'ii are illustrated with a "breath feather" (eagle down) on top of their heads. The name comes from the fact that eagle down is so light that the merest breath sets it in motion. Other feathers on the head are part of the physical attributes of each particular yé'ii.

The male holds a rattle and crooked lightning, while the female holds a rattle and evergreen boughs. Hanging from their wrists and elbows are fringe or ribbons. In ritual images, the rattles will always be held in their right hands and the evergreen or lightning in their left. The bulge on the calves indicates the direction from which the figure is moving. The skirt or kilt and the bag to the left of each yé'ii are the only two areas in ritual sandpaintings where the sandpainter is permitted to vary the design.

Variations not acceptable in ritual sandpaintings almost always appear in those made for sale. Knowledgeable—and cautious—artists deliberately make such changes to avoid creating an exact copy of a complete ritual sandpainting. (An exact image would summon the gods, something only an experienced hataałii should do and then only in the precisely structured confines of a Way.) Additionally, some artists will vary an element simply to make it fit their creative vision.

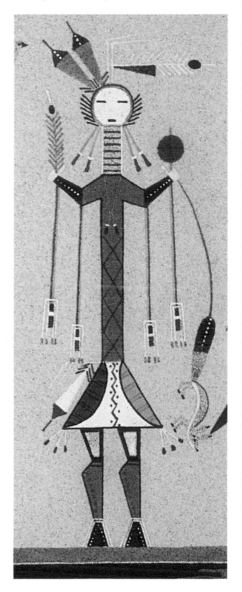

These two yé'ii are from a sandpainting by Joe Ben Jr.

25

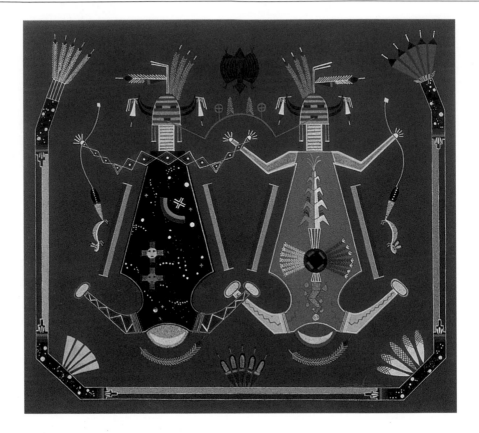

FATHER SKY (**Yádiłhił Ba'Hastíín**) and Mother Earth (**Nahasdzáánígíí**) appear in many sandpaintings of the Navajo Ways, including the Shooting Way, Mountain Way, and Blessing Way. They are invoked not because of their roles in a particular story, but because of their strength and all-pervading importance.

In the above image, artist Joe Ben portrays Father Sky and Mother Earth with banded faces and horns which symbolize their power. Father Sky is outlined in the white of dawn light, and Mother Earth is outlined in yellow pollen. In the body of Mother Earth are the four sacred plants: corn, beans, squash, and tobacco. (See page 47 for a discussion of the plants.) In the body of Father Sky are the constellations, including the Milky Way (**Łees'áán Yílzhódí**, which means literally "fluffy ashes") represented by the intertwined zigzag lines, along with the sun and moon. Constellations and stars important to the Navajo include

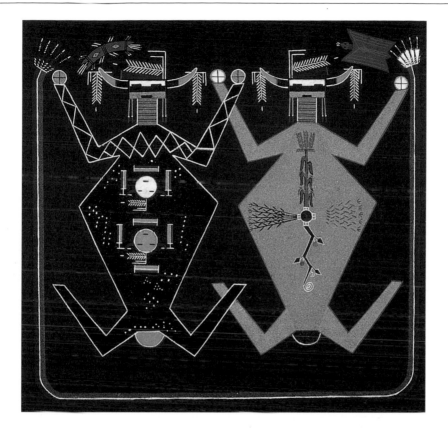

the yellow Coyote Star, Polaris, the Big Dipper (**Náhookǫs,** which is also the word for north), and the Pleiades. The guardian is the bat. Their arms and legs touch, just as the sky and the earth touch at the horizon. The encircling rainbow guardian ends with five eagle feathers on the right and five magpie feathers on the left.

In the other image, by George Joe, the faces are the traditional rectangular shape and banded with white for dawn, black for night, blue-gray for midday, and yellow (at the very bottom) for evening. They each hold symbols representing ceremonial baskets. Both a medicine bag and the bat are the guardians.

Artists frequently vary traditional sandpainting figures, the better pieces arising from an intimate knowledge of the Navajo religion while reflecting individual interpretation and experimentation with the forms.

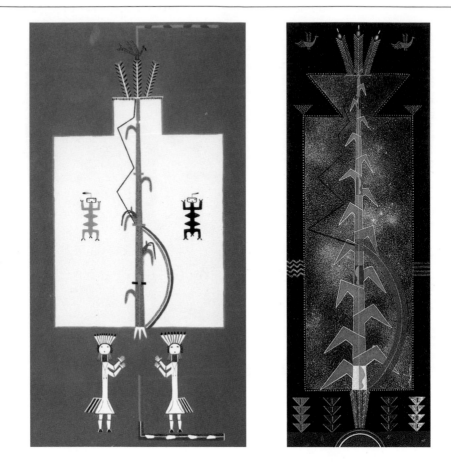

BOTH OF THESE SANDPAINTINGS are either directly from or based on a sequence used in the Blessing Way (**Hózhóójí**). Unlike the other ways, the Blessing Way is not a curing ritual. It may be held for the "coming of age" rite (**Kinaalda**) of young Navajo women, for pregnant women, at childbirth, at weddings, to stop disturbing dreams, to protect against harm or accident, to purify possessions, or to bless a house. In short, the Blessing Way secures a blessing at any point in life and ensures a long, good life. Navajos believe it to be the oldest of all their ceremonies and that it unifies all the others, for each Way ends with a song from the Blessing Way. Hataałii Long Moustache told ethnographer Father Berard Haile that the Blessing Way is the spinal column, or backbone, of their chants.

The Blessing Way was once a much longer observance, lasting up to five nights, but as of the turn of the twenty-first century, with its heavy demands from the secular world, the Blessing Way is generally a two-night ritual. The sandpainting reproduced here was originally the fourth in the series but now appears most often by itself in a one-day observance, sometimes referred to as a "no-sleep ceremony" because it includes all-night singing during which everyone is supposed to stay awake.

In the sandpainting on the left, east is to the right rather than at the top. The footprints on the lower rainbow represent the path of the people coming from one of the underworlds and passing between two figures called **Aȴkéé naa'aashii**, which translates as "Those who go together" or "Those who followed after one another." They are thought to be twins who were created in the Second World by a being named **Be'gochídí**, although much about them is either disputed or withheld by medicine men. As the rainbow path passes these two figures, it changes to yellow, representing corn pollen, and continues up the corn stalk alongside the female rainbow and the male lightning bolt, north to the yellow pollen footsteps at the top. The figures on either side of the corn are both Dontso (Big Fly). In ritual use, crushed flower petals and pollen are used in addition to crushed rock.

To the right is a sandpainting by Joe Ben Jr. that is inspired by Blessing Way images. He included lapis, a non-traditional material, along with traditional elements such as straight and crooked lightning and the four cloud motifs, to create this particularly dramatic combination of colors.

Thereby I became long life, thereby I became happiness,
May it be blessed before me, may it be blessed behind me,
May it be blessed below me, may it be blessed above me,
May it be blessed around me, may speech from me be blessed,
May all my surroundings be blessed.
It has become blessed again, it has become blessed again,
It has become blessed again, it has become blessed again.

—Portion of a prayer from the Blessing Way

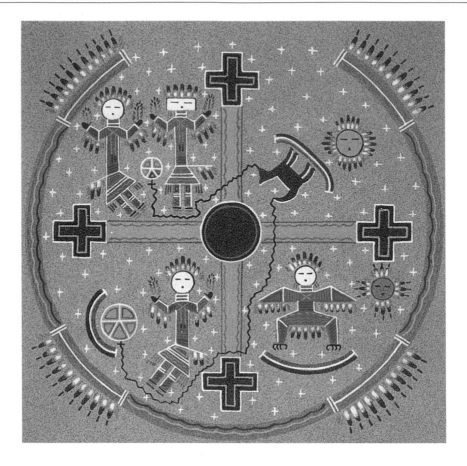

PART OF THE CREATION STORY recounts the time when First Man (**Átsé Hastiin**) and First Woman (**Átsé Asdzání**) had been transformed from ears of male white corn and female yellow corn and were living in their hogan, but living without fire. First Coyote (**Átsé' Hashké**) agreed to bring them some. He was quite afraid of the fire god, Black God (**Hashjesh-jin**), but nonetheless he proceeded on the long and arduous journey, relying upon his stealth and trickery to slip into Black God's hogan and steal a fiery brand to bring back to First Man and First Woman.

This traditional sandpainting shows First Coyote (also known as **Ma'ii** and He-Who-Wanders-About) as he is bringing back the fire. Black God is asleep with a medicine bag by his side and a feather in his left hand, where he should be holding a large ring of blue corn cakes. He is often portrayed with the fire drill he uses to make fire. Born to Comet Man and Fire Woman, he has zigzag lines representing the Milky Way across his arms and shoulders. He is credited with providing the light for the sun, moon, and stars of the Fourth World. The symbol beneath the medicine pouch is the fire itself, with a trail of embers leading away with First Coyote.

The little crosses represent stars and constellations. First Coyote and his red line of embers pass through the home of the Sun, with its eagle guardian in the lower right corner, then through the home of Moon in the upper right, and finally to the upper left home of First Man and First Woman. The large circles in the upper and lower left represent hogans, the traditional Navajo homes.

To the right is a contemporary, pictorial version of the same story. Here Coyote, Black God, as well as First Man and First Woman are portrayed not in their traditional stylized manner but in a more lifelike fashion. It becomes the visual equivalent of making a folktale out of a religious story.

I am the frivolous coyote
I wander about.
I have seen Hashjesh-jin's fire
I wander about.
I stole his fire from him
I wander about.
I have it! I have it!

—from the Creation Story

Monster Slayer, you are his child, he is your child.
First Man, you are his child, he is your child.
Born for Water, you are his child, he is your child.
First Woman, you are her child, she is your child.

–from the Creation Story

MONSTER SLAYER (**Nayéé' Neezghání**) may be identified by many names: Holy Man, Holy Boy, Changing Woman's Child, Changing Woman's Grandchild, among others. All are the same being, but the names emphasize different aspects of this important personality and his different functions or roles.

The sandpainting by Sammy Myerson on the left shows Monster Slayer standing against the sun as he appears in the Female Shooting Way. (The Shooting Way treats illnesses, including lung ailments, associated with thunder, lightning, and snakes, as well as illness caused by eating or drinking during an eclipse.) Here the sun is a pale grayish green, though pale blue may also be used. Monster Slayer is armed with crooked lightning given to him by his father the Sun. The Sun gave Monster Slayer's brother, Born for Water (**Tóbájíshchíní**), straight lightning. (The sandpainting titled Born for Water on the Moon also appears in the Shooting Way.) The serrated edges of his body indicate that he is wearing flint armor, also given to him by the Sun. He is surrounded by four eagles, each astride a rainbow bar which protects them and gives them greater power. The bow guardians and a garland of arrows protect the sandpainting as a whole.

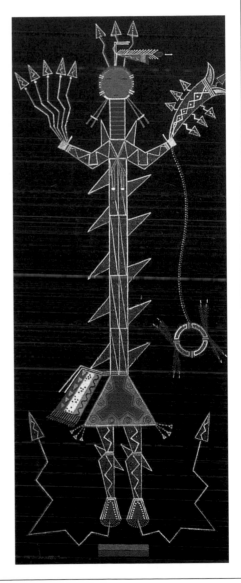

In the image by Joe Ben Jr. on the right, Monster Slayer holds a black hoop on a rope. In the Big Star Way (also known as the Great Star Chant) such hoops symbolize stars in a "hoop transformation" rite in which the patient passes through a succession of hoops, embellished with plants or herbs in a different color for each of the four directions, as a part of the healing process. When breath feathers are attached, the hoops represent a swift magical means of travel.

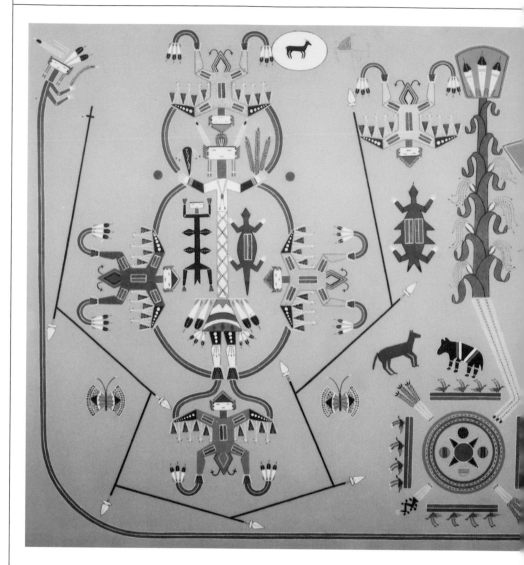

THIS UNUSUAL DOUBLE SANDPAINTING, made in the 1970s, comes from the
Shooting Way. The Navajo name for a double sandpainting translates as "facing
itself." Measuring 40 by 48 inches, this one is unusually large for a permanent
sandpainting. By contrast, those used in healing rites may be as large as 6 by 9 feet.

On the left is Holy Man, who went hunting with his brother, Holy Boy (on the
right). Holy Man shot a mountain sheep, shown in the white oval near the top,

with an arrow fletched with the wrong type of feathers. This angered the Thunder People, who then captured Holy Man with lightning bolts and took him up to the Sky People to be reprimanded and taught how to better use his power. Here we see Holy Man in the company of the two guardians, Big Fly and Otter (whose skin had protected him from the lightning), and surrounded by four Thunder People and a protective garland of arrows. The Thunder People taught Holy Man the ceremonies to cure illness caused by lightning, after which he went in search of his brother.

Holy Boy had gone in another direction and found a pool of water. In the middle of the pool was a reed with two eagle feathers attached to it. He tried to grab them three times and three times missed. On the fourth try he fell into the water and was swallowed by a huge fish that took him down to the home of the Water People. The fish is painted on all four sides of Holy Boy, whose upper torso is surrounded by a star symbolizing his having been swallowed. Although it may look more like a horned lizard at first, the figure is indeed a fish with fins on each side and a forked tail behind. The addition of hands and legs may surprise a non-Navajo, who may not at first think of fish as "Fish People."

In Holy Boy's right hand is the flint knife he used to cut his way out of the fish. The corn plant at his side is not as much a part of the story as it is a part of the Shooting Way ceremony, in which the patient is given a medicine made of fish blood and corn pollen rolled into a little ball. The Water People were very angry at Big Fish for bringing an "earth person" among them, until Big Fly came and told them that the intruder was Holy Boy. They then taught him prayers, songs, and sandpaintings to cure illness caused by water. The image is also part of the Plume, or Feather, Way.

One of the Thunders who found Holy Boy is also here, along with a bear and a wolf who helped look for the missing Twin, as did the ducks below them. In the traditional Shooting Way sandpainting, the four groups of four ducks would have rainbow loops at their bills to carry lightning.

BÍÍGHÁÁ'ASK'IDII (previously written as B'ganaskiddy) is known in English by a variety of names: Humpbacked Yé'ii, Hunchback Yé'ii, God of Plenty, God of the Mist, Harvest God, or the misnomer "Camel God," which he is not. The hump on his back is actually a deerskin bag painted black with eagle (some say woodpecker) feathers attached. The short white stripes are the seeds that Bíígháá'ask'idii is carrying in the bag, said to represent the seeds of all plants. This sandpainting correctly portrays the Bíígháá'ask'idii with mountain sheep horns, which many fail to include. Sometimes they can be seen holding a staff or a water jug enclosed in a net. These two flank a corn plant.

Bíígháá'ask'idii is an important figure in the Night Way ceremony, used to treat a range of maladies including nervousness and insanity. In this chant, the hero is tracking mountain sheep. He locates four of them, but each time they pass he cannot shoot because his fingers have frozen to the arrow. After the fourth failure the mountain sheep reveal themselves as gods: four Bíígháá'ask'idii. They transform him into a mountain sheep as well and take him home to teach him the curing rites that make up part of the Night Way.

THERE WAS ONCE A MONSTER named **Tsenahyeh** (Traveling Rock), who would crush those who came near him. When Monster Slayer came to destroy him, Tsenahyeh hid on the bottom of a lake. Three times Monster Slayer tried to destroy him and three times Tsehnayeh escaped. On the fourth time, Monster Slayer finally spotted him under the water and with his stone club struck him into many pieces. That is how **Téholtsódii** (Water Creature) came to be. Téholtsódii was then instructed to make the rivers flow and henceforth be responsible for them.

In another legend from the Creation Story, Téholtsódii began to flood the Third World, forcing everyone to flee up to the Fourth World. Still the waters rose, coming after them. They held a conference and discovered that Coyote was the culprit, having stolen and hidden Téholtsódii's child. (In some versions, it's two children.) As soon as Coyote was forced to return the child, throwing him into the water at the Emergence Hole, the waters subsided.

This example is artist Red Goat's own interpretation of Téholtsódii, with an inset of turquoise stones. He has used cloud symbols for the hands and feet and has set Water Creature against a background of several guardian figures. Images of Water Creature can be found in sandpaintings from the Water Way, Shooting Way, Beauty Way, and Plume Way.

DUE TO A MISTAKE in the titling of this image in a mid twentieth-century publication, Pollen Boy on the Sun is sometimes referred to as Eagle on the Sun, a complete misnomer as there is no such sandpainting. Pollen Boy (called **Tádídíín 'Ashkii**) on the Sun is an image used in the Shooting Way and the Chiricahua Wind Way. If done for a boy, it includes the four sacred plants. If done for a man, the plants are absent. Each cardinal direction is represented with twelve feathers colored for the appropriate direction (white for the east, red for the south, yellow for the west, and black for the north), mirroring the four sets of twelve songs from the ceremony. Pollen Boy symbolizes the male aspect of life generation and is never outlined when appearing in the ritual image.

The sandpainting to the right is an image of Corn Beetle Girl, or **Trahdah-de'en-ahtehd** on the Moon, used in ceremonies for women. (Most chants have female and male versions.) The Moon, or **Klayonaheh**, is always white; here she is shown with the ceremonial horned headdress. Crooked and straight lightning emanate from each of her four sides and are in turn encircled by protective rainbow bars. Like Pollen Boy, Corn Beetle Girl is always a solid color, with no outlining. She is credited with giving most beings their voice. Despite the English translation of her name, which is better translated as an insect called Corn Ripener, she is also thought of as pollen personified in Navajo religion.

Both Pollen Boy and Corn Beetle Girl are important beings in the Blessing Way sandpaintings and generally appear together, often with Changing Woman who, among many other aspects, represents the earth and personifies the seasons. The pollen that the three represent has been called "a symbol of fertility, happiness, and life itself" by anthropologist Leland Wyman. Both sandpaintings are by Joe Ben Jr.

> *My feet are all sorts of pollen, it shows my way;*
> *My legs are all sorts of pollen, it shows my way;*
> *My body are all sorts of pollen, it shows my way;*
> *My thoughts are all sorts of pollen, it shows my way;*
> *My voice is all sorts of pollen, it shows my way;*
> *My feather are all sorts of pollen, it shows my way;*
> *I am covered with all sorts of pollen, it shows my way....*
> *Behind me, it is beautiful, it shows my way;*
> *Behind me, it is beautiful, it shows my way.*
>
> —from the Creation Story

THIS SANDPAINTING IS FROM the Hail Way (**Níló-jí**), which is no longer held, for no living hataałii knows it. The last medicine man to perform it was Hosteen Klah, who knew an incredible total of six Ways. Fortunately, Klah had the foresight to see that most of the ceremony was recorded.

In both the old example by James Joe and the new version by Sammy Meyerson on the right, we see the heads of two rows of figures holding up the night. In the traditional example, the white line around the edge of the night represents the dawn. Within the body of both paintings are the various constellations, placed in the sky by Black God, Hashjesh-jin. Among them is Náhookos, known in English as the Big Dipper. The intertwined zigzag lines represent the Milky Way (Łees'áán Yílzhódí), the horned heads the sun and moon.

A portion of the Navajo Creation Story tells how the stars were being positioned in the sky in an orderly fashion to form the constellations we recognize today. Coyote begged to be allowed to help, but his reputation as an incompetent fool who usually failed to follow directions had preceded him. Undeterred by First Woman's refusal, Coyote managed to sneak over and grab the bag of stars before they all had been placed. As he raced away, he stumbled

and the bag fell open. The remaining stars flew up into the heavens willy-nilly. The oral traditions of other Southwest Indian tribes contain similar stories.

Around the upper and lower edges of both sandpaintings are a number of guardians. Beginning with the top left and going sunwise (clockwise) in the James Joe version, they are Mountain Bluebird, Yellow-shouldered Blackbird, Yellow Warbler, Western Tanager, Mountain Sheep (who looks more like a coyote in these versions), Western Bluebird, and Bat (the messenger of the night), who is shown on a bed of pollen.

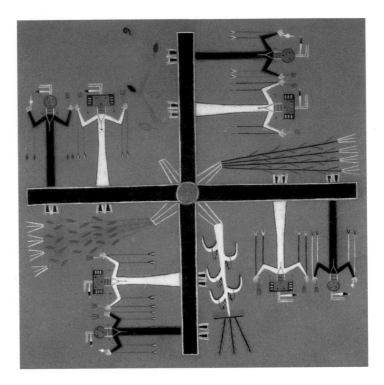

THE WHIRLING LOGS, or **Tsil'ol-ni**, story occurs in both the Night Way and Feather Way, as well as another version that occurs in the Chiricahua Wind Way. The hero of the story, named Self Teacher, decides to leave home because his family is angry at him for his gambling losses. So he sets out on a long journey.

At first the gods try to persuade him not to go. But seeing his determination, they help him hollow out a log in which he travels down the river with his pet turkey (which followed him to the river bank, as do the gods). He and his craft are captured by Water Monster, who carries him down beneath the waters of the river to the home of the Water People. The gods have difficulty rescuing him until Black God threatens to set fire to Water Monster's home, forcing him to release the hero. Before the hero is released, Frog teaches Self Teacher how to cure the illnesses caused by the Water People. When Self Teacher's whirling log finally arrives at the lake (or in some versions, a whirlpool) that was his destination, Talking God, Hastye Hogan, and two Bíígháá'ask'idii rescue him.

The final surprise comes when the hero is reunited with his pet turkey, which shakes its wings, releasing the seeds put there by the gods. Self Teacher then plants a field of crops that quickly ripen for harvest. He returns home to share the knowledge of farming that he has gained and the cures that he has learned.

The icon of the whirling logs has no connection to the old European design of a Greek cross with bent arms, the well-known symbol used by the German Nazis, or the ancient Buddhist symbol (often used to denote a sacred site). Some Navajos have said that nineteenth-century traders introduced it for use in rug and jewelry designs. Its use by tribes of the American Southwest, from the Tohono O'odham and Hopi to the Navajo and Apache, largely ended with the advent of World War II.

In the image at left created by Fred Stevens in 1964, the logs are outlined in white to represent the foam of the water, with yellow for pollen on the water. Figures in sandpaintings generally proceed clockwise, hence the positioning of the yé'ii figures. The second image is more unusual. Since about 1990, Navajo "folk art" tradition has begun to draw on more traditional roots. Here the Whirling Logs story has inspired Thomas Begay Jr. to interpret the legend in wood.

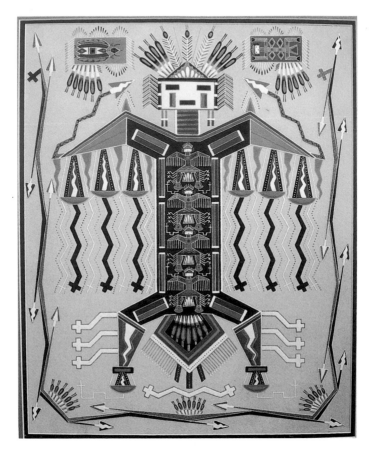

THE THUNDER PEOPLE are very powerful and therefore potentially very dangerous. They should not be confused with the Thunderbird, which is a part of Pueblo and Plains Indian traditions, not the Navajo religion.

Above is Big Thunder (**Ii'ni' Tsoh**), as portrayed by Joe Ben, with lightning issuing from his wings and feet. The many rainbow bars show Big Thunder's great strength. In his body are four thunders of the four directions. Pink Thunder (of the north) is generally not portrayed as it is too dangerous a being to call into a sandpainting. The lightning lines issuing from Big Thunder's wings represent white female and black male lightning. Bat and Dontso are the guardians, and lightning forms the protective garland. The weasel headdress

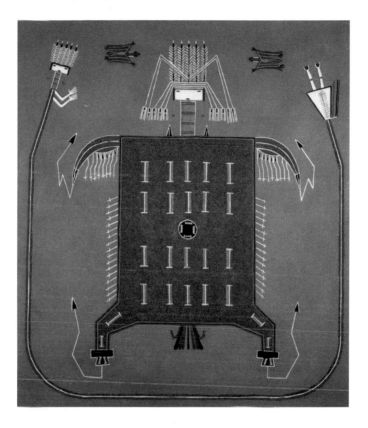

indicates that this sandpainting is part of the Mountain Way. The smaller thunder figure on the right is a more commonly seen representation of the Thunder People, done in the 1970s.

Ii'ni' Tsoh is generally regarded as a dangerous if not downright malevolent being, although a thunder can also have the power to find missing objects. Thunders appear in as many as eight ways, according to some experts. In the Hail Way, the hero Rain Boy is destroyed by Winter Thunder but is ultimately rescued by the Thunder People, who gather up his remains in a sacred buckskin. The Winds then restore his movement, the Insect People find and bring back some of his blood, and Talking God uses pollen to recreate his body hair, toenails, and fingernails. Sun restores his vision, and the Spider People restore his blood vessels and nerves. (In another Way, the Wind People have to be called to make his nerves function again.)

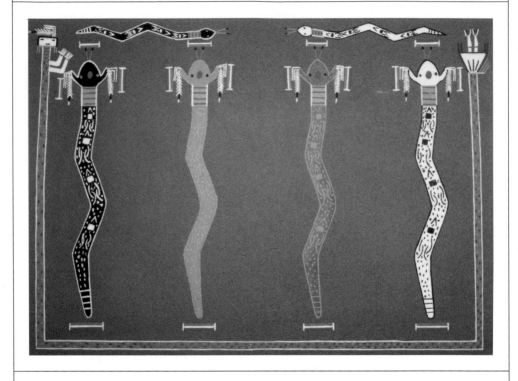

THE NAVAJOS HAVE LONG ASSOCIATED snakes with lightning because of their shape and speed. Both are feared because of their great power. This is a sandpainting of the Snake People, whose yellow fangs indicate that they are not poisonous. Red fangs would indicate poison.

Big Snake Man is a snake being usually illustrated with a horned headdress indicating power and eagle plumes representing speed. In one story, the hero uses poisonous tobacco to overcome Big Snake and render him unconscious. Big Snake's wife pleads with the hero to restore her husband in exchange for all their valuables. After doing so, the hero trades the valuables back to Big Snake for the ceremonial knowledge and sandpaintings, which he had come seeking in the first place.

Generally speaking, among Snake People (who may also appear in quasi-human form) male snakes are represented in zigzag shapes and female as straight. Slender snakes, which probably represent racer snakes, are sometimes called arrow snakes and appear in the Bead Way. Whirling Snakes appear in the Shooting Way.

THE FOUR SACRED PLANTS in the Navajo system are the bean (**naa'ołí**), corn (**naadą́ą́'**), tobacco (**nát'oh**), and squash (**naaghízí**). Their representation is a fundamental theme in whole or in part in many sandpaintings. This one presents three of those plants. Beginning at the top right and going clockwise are bean, corn, corn again, and squash. In a traditional painting, a tobacco plant would replace the second stalk of corn. In sandpainting imagery, tobacco is drawn much like the bean plant but without the dots. The plants may be shown in plant or human form, but either way they are recognized as being the sacred plants.

The frogs indicate that this sandpainting is intended to treat someone crippled, paralyzed, or with arthritis. The Water People are thought to be the cause of such illnesses. The white and yellow frogs are female frogs of the east and west, while the black and blue-gray are male frogs representing the north. This sandpainting was made by Fred Stevens in about 1965.

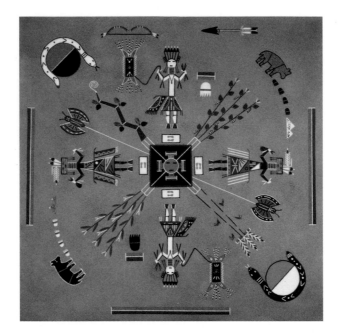

THIS THEME OCCURS IN BOTH the Beauty Way and the Mountain Way, but the story has its origins in yet another ceremonial—the Blessing Way. Big Snake Man and Bear Man, disguised as very old men, compete successfully in a battle against the Pueblo People and then in archery contests against Monster Slayer and his companions. The reward for the winners is supposed to be two beautiful maidens, illustrated here as the two square-headed female figures at the right and left. Although the two old men win every contest Monster Slayer can think of, Monster Slayer chooses to deny them their prize, much to the relief of the girls.

That night, while the others attend a social dance, Big Snake Man and Bear Man transform themselves into rich, handsome young men. Using a sweet-smelling magic tobacco, they lure the girls to them. Upon awakening in the morning, the maidens find that the young men have changed back into the old men they had spurned the day before. Frightened, they flee. Big Snake Man's pursuit of one of the maidens continues in the Beauty Way, while Bear Man's chase is a part of the Mountain Way.

The butterflies in the sandpainting symbolize the beauty of the maidens, and the bear tracks represent their pursuers. The snakes are shown in their hogans

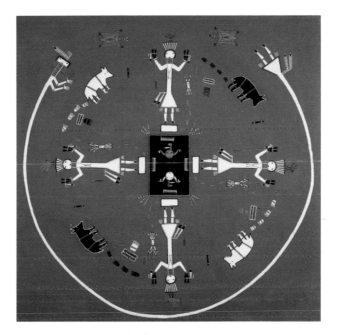

in opposite corners and the bears near their mountain homes. The two figures at the top and bottom are both **Yáshti' Yé'ii**, each one holding a medicine bag in his right hand. This figure is usually referred to as Grandfather of the Gods or Talking God, although a more appropriate translation would be Speechless Talking One, for he is one of a small group of gods who no longer speak as they did in times long past. He has control over the eastern sky, dawn, corn, and large game animals. Of all the Holy People, he is regarded as being the most compassionate. Yáshti' Yé'ii also appears in the Night Way.

In the sandpainting above, Bear Man is in pursuit of the maiden alone. The bar in front of each bear represents the pipe of special tobacco which helps Bear Man find her. The four white figures are Yáshti' Yé'ii.

> *I, I am Talking God, now I wander about.*
> *From under the East I wander about, now I wander about.*
> *The dawn lies toward me, I wander about, now I wander about.*
> *The white corn lies toward me, now I wander about.*
>
> —from the Night Way

THE TWIN WAR GODS

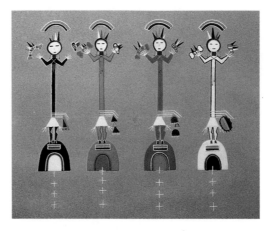

THIS IMAGE WAS USED for those about to go into battle against an enemy for the first time. The hataałii who helped record the image for posterity, Jeff King, said it was to "protect the whole Navajo tribe." On the white mountain of the East stands Monster Slayer, on the yellow mountain of the South stands Born for Water, on the blue mountain of the West is Reared in the Earth, and Changing Grandchild stands atop the black mountain of the North. (See the facing page for a complete list of the mountains in Navajo and English.)

Reared in the Earth, Changing Grandchild, Second Born, Came Down on a Sunbeam, Holy Man, and Holy Boy are all different manifestations of the Twin War Gods.

> *In the Place of the Emergence,*
> *In the place where they came up,*
> *In the holy mountains,*
> *In the place where the people*
> *Came up from the lower world to this world,*
> *There were four mountains coming up.*
> *There, in the north, a black mountain standing,*
> *In the east, a white mountain standing,*
> *In the south, a blue mountain standing*
> *In the west, a yellow mountain standing,*
> *And a god is standing on each mountaintop.*

—from The Two Who Went to Their Father

HERE THE TWIN WAR GODS (who appear to be upside down) stand on a rainbow at the edge of Hot Spring Lake. Around them are the four mountains that mark the traditional boundaries of Dinétah (Navajoland).

East: the white **Yoolgai Dzilo** is usually White Shell Mountain, known also as Sierra Blanca Peak, located in the section of the Sangre de Cristo Mountains that stretch up into southern Colorado. Yoolgai Dzilo is often associated with White Shell Woman and the substance of sacred white shell itself.

South: **Tsoodzil**, or Tongue Mountain (popularly known as Mt. Taylor), is located in the San Mateo Range of western New Mexico and is associated with turquoise.

West: **Dook'o'osɬííd**, known as Humphrey's Peak in the San Francisco Peaks near Flagstaff, Arizona, is often associated with abalone. Its name reflects some of the quality of the pearly color in its meaning, "light shines from it." In rituals it is addressed as Abalone Mountain.

North: **Dibé'ntsé** means literally Sheep Rock Mountain and is known in English as Hesperus Peak, in the La Plata Mountains of southwestern Colorado.

In this sandpainting, used for men about to go to war (as was Mountain Around Which Moving Was Done) and for protection from people who think ill of you, the Twin War Gods are wearing the armor and carrying the weapons that their father gave them. The rainbow bars are for the protection and strength of the mountains themselves.

THIS SANDPAINTING IS CALLED The Buffalo Who Never Die, a title that came from the story of a man who married the daughter of the chief of the Buffalo People, the **Ayání** (more accurately known as bison). When the Buffalo People returned to their home on the Plains, he was told not to follow. But of course, he did. When the Buffalo People discovered him, they decided to kill him. The yé'ii had warned the man of this, so he was armed with special magic which they had taught him. He killed the Buffalo People instead, but eventually revived them in exchange for certain ceremonial knowledge. In the Creation Story these beings are said to be the offspring of Buffalo Woman and Holy Man.

The detail (by Rosie Yellowhair) is one of the Buffalo People who were restored to life, symbolized by the rainbow belt around his middle. At his side is the Plains-style medicine hoop that the hero used to resuscitate the Buffalo. The bison in both sandpaintings are stylized, with their shaggy manes looking more like those of horses, sometimes confusing viewers who may not immediately recognize the horns on their heads. In the larger image, by Michael Tsosie, the tepees represent the home of the Buffalo People to the east on the Great Plains. Often sandpainters will

add white lines from the bison to the center of the sandpainting, representing their trails to water. Traditionally they have a yellow pollen line on their bellies, the pollen of the plants they run through. With a lone exception in the Plume Way, the Buffalo People appear only in the Shooting Way. In some images they have human heads and arms and hold medicine hoops.

THESE ARE THE RAINBOW PEOPLE (Nááts'íílid Yé'ii) who usually appear in pairs, much as rainbows do in nature. They appear in the Mountain Way, Male Shooting Way, Blessing Way, Night Way, and Wind Way, among other ceremonies. The four sacred plants represent the Rainbow People's association with water.

This sandpainting depicts four Rainbow People by Kee Silversmith swirling in dynamic curves around the Place of Emergence. Here the holy water is a four-colored circle enclosing the four cloud symbols. The four corner elements, suggestive of cloud motifs, are purely decorative.

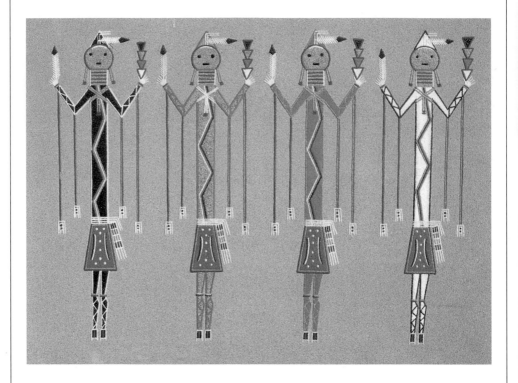

IN THIS IMAGE by Fred Stevens each of the four **Niltsi Yé'ii**, or Wind People, are a different color representing the four directions. In one hand they hold cloud symbols, and in the other they hold the feather that is used to create the winds. The Wind People are very important in Navajo legends since they were the ones who relayed the ceremonial knowledge from the Holy People to the Navajos.

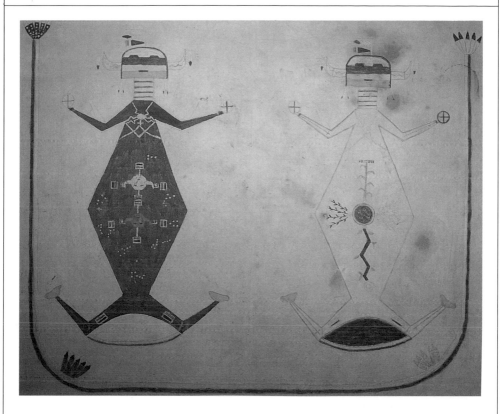

DESPITE THE NAME and the story that first circulated when these appeared, Navajo hataałii did not make or keep images to help them remember the details of their many sandpaintings. An early ethnographer came across one hataałii using such 'crib sheets' but found that other hataałii regarded it as a sign of failing memory or incompetence. The one reproduced here shows Father Sky and Mother Earth painted on cloth in the early 1980s by Bruce Hatahal.

Still life by Eugene Baatsoslanii Joe

A NUMBER OF CONTEMPORARY sandpainting artists have developed not only their own artistic styles but new techniques, along with new materials. Following the technical lead of Eugene Baatsoslanii Joe, they literally paint with sand, creating shadows, textures, and a sense of depth. Their work has received international recognition from Japan to Northern Europe.

Eugene Baatsoslanii Joe was the first of the contemporary Navajo sandpainting artists to show his work outside the United States. He has created not only portraits and realistic landscapes (see his yé'ii bichai dancer on page 10), but still life images as well. His work is noteworthy for the use of perspective, shadowing, and highlights—the latter two extremely difficult to master with sand and glue. Here he has combined a portrayal of a decorated pot with a Navajo rug of the traditional Two Grey Hills design, turned back to reveal a butterfly, a Navajo symbol of beauty.

In the sandpainting of a Navajo weaver and her granddaughter, artist Little River has used crushed turquoise for the stones in the bracelet and a silver-colored sand for the bracelets themselves. The weaver appears to be working on a yé'ii rug.

A Navajo weaver and her grandchild, by Little River

EMERGENCE STORY OF THE FIVE WORLDS

OTHER ARTISTS ARE TACKLING very complex subjects. The image on the left is a pictorial representation of the Navajo creation story as conceived by Rosie Yellowhair, who entitled it Emergence Story of the Five Worlds. Precise details of the Emergence Story vary between clans. Even the exact number of worlds may vary (from four to sixteen), but the fundamental narrative remains unchanged.

With some visual embellishment here, the basic version begins with the First World, sometimes called the Red World or the Black World, which was a disagreeably cold, dark, and wet place populated only by twelve insect beings and four monsters who lived in the surrounding ocean. The Insect People included ants, beetles, locusts, and bats. According to several versions, there was only one word in the whole world, which meant peacefulness. But in time there was also dissension and witchcraft. The Insect People were then advised by Water Creature to fly to the world above them.

Through a small opening the Insect People entered the muddy Second World, a wide barren plain which was the home of the Swallow People. This Second World was blue. There was peace for a time until dissension arose again and the Swallow People ordered the Insect People to leave. So they flew up to the sky but had great trouble locating an opening into the next world. Finally it was found—a tiny slit in the southern sky. They arrived in the Third (or Yellow) World with difficulty and found themselves in the land of the Grasshopper People, through which a stream flowed. So the Locust and other Insect People settled with the Grasshopper People, but again it wasn't long before dissension arose and the Insect People had to leave. Some of the Grasshopper People came with them.

This time it was extremely hard finding the place to enter the Fourth World. They had almost given up when they saw the head of a bird poking through the western sky. They made their way through the hole into a world of black and white and were astounded to find four great mountains anchoring the world. Much happened to them in this world, for it was here that the Animal People lived. The Animal People taught the newcomers how to farm, and it was here that people saw the first yé'ii—Talking God, Water Bearer, Hogan God, and Black God. The yé'ii stayed for four days instructing the people in the ways of the Holy

People. Black God stayed behind when the other three left. When the other yé'ii returned, they held a ritual in which an ear of white corn was transformed into a man and an ear of yellow corn into a woman. So First Man and First Woman were born, and the Holy Winds breathed the life force into them.

The new beings were instructed in how to live, from singing the sacred songs to planting and weaving. They multiplied rapidly and for a time all was well. But then Coyote (illustrated here in a form that more closely resembles a fox) stole Water Creature's child, and Water Creature was so enraged that he began to flood the world. The people fled to the mountaintops, but the floodwaters came after them. A succession of birds went in search of an opening in the sky and finally found one, but how would all the Animals and other People get through in time? The Squirrel People managed to grow a juniper tree and a piñon tree extremely high but not high enough. The Weasel People planted a pine and a spruce, but they, too, were not high enough. At last an old man planted a reed which grew right up into the next world, and all the people climbed through. In one version of the story, Coyote—the guilty party—was the first to enter, while turkey—his feathers filled with seeds of corn, beans, squash, and melons—was the last. The foaming white floodwaters touched his tail, turning the tips of his feathers white. Bobcat, Badger, Bear, and even Coyote helped enlarge the opening into the Fifth, or White World. Most versions mention that while many witches were destroyed in the flood, at least one escaped into the Fifth World, which explains the presence of evil today.

Many of these elements are present in Rosie Yellowhair's version of the story, including the four sacred mountains of Dinetah, Coyote stealing and spilling the stars, the Milky Way, two Thunders, and the corn motif that is central to the Blessing Way.

CONTEMPORARY THEMES

In response to market demands, some Navajo artists have begun to use other tribal subjects in their sandpaintings. The artist Kee Silversmith has combined Navajo, Hopi, and Rio Grande Pueblo symbols, objects, and designs into the lower sandpainting, while artist Joe Ben Jr. has worked with abstractions of primarily Navajo imagery. Joe Ben has also achieved widespread recognition for work that incorporates a number of minerals and semi-precious stones not used

An unusually shaped sandpainting by Joe Ben Jr.

before in Navajo sandpainting art. Ben's work has explored subjects from a more conceptual and abstract point of view. In this extraordinary piece he has achieved effects with sand and glue normally associated with the medium of watercolor.

An untitled contemporary design by Kee Silversmith

LANDSCAPES

More and more Navajo sandpainting artists are veering away from traditional religious symbols to portray non-religious subjects, most notably landscapes that include enduring features of Navajo daily life, using the techniques developed in sandpainting. Here are two such seasonal scenes of the Navajo Reservation, in the remarkably beautiful Four Corners region now famous all over the world. The winter scene is by War Eagle, the farming scene by Little River. Both include hogans and the ramadas usually used as summer kitchens.

YÉ'II RHYTHM

A number of artists use non-specific yé'ii images, that is, figures that in form and appearance are based upon the attributes or appearance of yé'iis but are not the true spirit beings. This image by Daniel Smith incorporates such designs, along with animal and geometric features that work together to create a rhythm that is the visual equivalent of the chants which accompany the creation of the religious sandpaintings.

DECORATIVE ITEMS

Some sandpainting artists have turned their skills to décor items, including nameplates, boxes, lamps, clocks, and signs. Most of these pieces are sold unsigned in trading posts and other retail stores throughout the Southwest.

SUGGESTED READING

Bahti, Tom. *Southwestern Indian Ceremonials*. Las Vegas: K.C. Publications, 1970.

Farella, John R. *The Main Stalk: A Synthesis of Navajo Philosophy*. Tucson: University of Arizona Press, 1984.

Faris, James C. *The Night Way: A History and Documentation of a Navajo Ceremonial*. Albuquerque: University of New Mexico Press, 1990.

Foster, Kenneth E. *Navajo Sandpaintings*. Window Rock, AZ: Navajo Tribal Museum, 1964.

Frisbie, Charlotte J. *Kinaaldá: A Study of the Navajo Girl's Puberty Ceremony*. Original edition, 1967. Reprint, Salt Lake City: University of Utah Press, 1993.

Griffen-Pierce, Trudy. *Earth is My Mother, Sky is My Father: Space, Time and Astronomy in Navajo Sandpainting*. Albuquerque: University of New Mexico Press, 1995.

Matthews, Washington. "Mythic Dry-paintings of the Navajo." *The American Naturalist* 19, no. 10, 1884.

McCoy, Ronald. *Summoning the Gods: Sandpainting in the Native American Southwest. Plateau* 59, no. 1, 1988.

Newcomb, Franc J., and Gladys Reichard. Original edition, 1937. *Sandpaintings of the Navajo Shooting Chant*. Reprint, New York: Dover Publications, 1975.

Parezo, Nancy J. *Navajo Sandpaintings: From Religion to Commercial Art*. Albuquerque: University of New Mexico Press, 1991.

Reichard, Gladys A. *Navajo Medicine Man Sandpaintings*. Original edition, 1939. Reprint, New York: Dover Publications, 1975.

Reichard, Gladys. *Navaho Religion: A Study of Symbolism*. Original edition, 1950. Reprint, Tucson: University of Arizona Press, 1983.

Wyman, Leland C. *Blessingway*. Tucson: University of Arizona Press, 1970.

————. *Mountain Way of the Navajo*. Tucson: University of Arizona Press, 1975.

————. *Navaho Sandpainting: The Huckel Collection*. Colorado Springs, CO: Taylor Museum, 1964.

Zolbrod, Paul G. *Diné Bahane': The Navajo Creation Story*. Albuquerque: University of New Mexico Press, 1984.

ABOUT THE AUTHOR

MARK BAHTI grew up in the Indian arts business, accompanying his father, the late Tom Bahti, on frequent trips to the reservations in the Southwest. He has written widely on the subject and is the author of *Spirit in the Stone: A Handbook of Southwest Indian Animal Carvings and Beliefs* and *Pueblo Stories and Storytellers*. He has long been active in organizations to promote Indian arts, education, and economic development. He runs Bahti Indian Arts in Tucson and is also a Fellow of the Society for Applied Anthropology.